"Mastering Online Business: A Comprehensive Guide to Success"

Table of Contents:

I0454564

Introduction

Welcome to "**Mastering Online Business: A Comprehensive Guide to Success**"! In the ever-evolving landscape of business, the shift toward online platforms has become not just a trend, but a necessity for entrepreneurs and visionaries. The digital era has ushered in unparalleled opportunities, and the key to unlocking them lies in mastering the realm of online business.

In today's fast-paced world, establishing a robust online presence is not merely a choice; it is a strategic imperative. Whether you are an aspiring entrepreneur, a small business owner, or someone looking to expand your ventures into the digital space, this guide is your compass to navigate the exciting and dynamic world of online business.

The Power of Online Business

The digital revolution has redefined the way we connect, consume, and conduct business. The rise of new technologies and the ubiquity of social media have dismantled geographical barriers, opening doors to a global marketplace. Online business offers a level playing field, allowing individuals and enterprises of all sizes to compete and thrive.

Why Go Online?

1. Global Reach: Reach customers beyond borders and tap into diverse markets.
2. Cost-Efficiency: Reduce overhead costs associated with brick-and-mortar establishments.
3. Flexibility: Operate 24/7, providing convenience to customers across different time zones.
4. Data-Driven Insights: Leverage analytics to understand customer behaviour and refine strategies.
5. Social Media Influence: Harness the power of social media to connect, engage, and build a brand community.

Embracing Change

As we delve into this guide, you will discover practical insights, actionable strategies, and real-world examples to empower you on your online business journey. From finding your niche to scaling your operations, each chapter is crafted to equip you with the knowledge and tools needed to thrive in the digital age.

The future of business is digital, and the possibilities are limitless. Whether you're starting from scratch or looking to elevate your existing online presence, this guide is your roadmap to success. Let's embark on this transformative journey together and master the art of online business.

Are you ready to turn your entrepreneurial dreams into reality? Let's dive in!

Chapter 1: Understanding Online Business
Section 1: Introduction to Online Business

Definition of Online Business

In the dynamic landscape of commerce, the term "online business" refers to a mode of conducting commercial activities that primarily takes place over the internet. Unlike traditional brick-and-mortar establishments, online businesses leverage digital platforms to reach, engage, and transact with their audience.

Key Characteristics of Online Business:

1. Digital Presence: Online businesses operate in the virtual realm, establishing a digital storefront through websites, e-commerce platforms, and other online channels.

2. E-Commerce Transactions: The core of online business often involves the buying and selling of goods or services through electronic transactions, facilitated by secure payment gateways.

3. Digital Marketing: Online businesses employ digital marketing strategies to promote their products or services, leveraging channels such as social media, search engines, and email.

4. Global Accessibility: One of the defining features of online business is its potential for global reach. Through the internet, businesses can transcend geographical boundaries and connect with a diverse, international audience.

Forms of Online Business:

1. E-Commerce Stores: Retailers and entrepreneurs can set up virtual stores to sell a wide range of products directly to consumers.

2. Digital Services: Many businesses offer digital services such as online consulting, digital marketing, software development, and more.

3. Affiliate Marketing: Some online businesses generate revenue through affiliate marketing, where they promote and sell products on behalf of other companies for a commission.

4. Subscription Models: Businesses may adopt subscription models, providing ongoing services or content in exchange for recurring payments.

Evolution of Online Business:

The roots of online business trace back to the emergence of the internet, gaining momentum with the proliferation of e-commerce platforms in the late 20th century. Since then, the landscape has evolved rapidly, incorporating advanced technologies, mobile commerce, and sophisticated digital marketing strategies.

In the contemporary era, online business is not just a supplementary model; it is a fundamental aspect of the global economy. The advent of social media, advanced analytics, and secure online transactions has transformed the way businesses operate and interact with consumers.

Why Online Business Matters:

The significance of online business extends beyond the convenience it offers to consumers. It provides businesses with unprecedented opportunities for growth, cost-effectiveness, and the ability to adapt to rapidly changing market trends. For entrepreneurs and established businesses alike, embracing online business is not merely a strategic choice; it is an essential step toward staying competitive in the digital age.

As we delve deeper into this guide, you'll gain a more comprehensive understanding of the intricacies of online business—from its advantages and challenges to practical strategies for success.

Evolution of Online Business:

Early Beginnings: The Emergence of E-Commerce
The evolution of online business traces its roots to the early days of the internet, where the concept of conducting commercial transactions electronically began to take shape. In the 1970s and 1980s, electronic data interchange (EDI) systems allowed businesses to exchange information and conduct transactions electronically. However, it was the advent of the World Wide Web in the 1990s that truly revolutionized the landscape.

1990s: The Rise of E-Commerce Platforms

The 1990s marked a pivotal era with the establishment of the first e-commerce platforms. Companies like Amazon and eBay emerged, laying the foundation for online retail. These platforms facilitated secure online transactions, transforming the way consumers shopped and businesses operated. The dot-com boom witnessed a surge in online businesses, although many were met with challenges, leading to the dot-com bust at the turn of the century.

2000s: *Technological Advancements and Digital Marketing*

The 2000s witnessed significant technological advancements that propelled the growth of online business. The widespread adoption of high-speed internet, coupled with improved security measures, made online transactions more seamless and secure. Digital marketing strategies, including search engine optimization (SEO) and pay-per-click (PPC) advertising, gained prominence, allowing businesses to reach their target audiences with unprecedented precision.

2010s: *Mobile Commerce and Social Media Influence*

The proliferation of smartphones in the 2010s brought about a new era in online business—mobile commerce. Consumers could now shop, interact, and conduct transactions anytime, anywhere. Social media platforms emerged as powerful tools for businesses to connect with their audience, build brand communities, and leverage user-generated content. The rise of influencer marketing further reshaped how products and services were promoted online.

Current Significance: Online Business in the Digital Age

In the present day, online business is not just a facet of commerce; it is the heartbeat of the global economy. The COVID-19 pandemic underscored the resilience of online business models, with e-commerce experiencing unprecedented growth as traditional businesses adapted to the challenges of lockdowns and social distancing. Online platforms have become integral to the daily lives of consumers, offering convenience, choice, and accessibility.

Key Significance Points:

1. Global Connectivity: Online business has bridged geographical gaps, enabling businesses to operate on a global scale and consumers to access products and services from around the world.

2. Diverse Business Models: From e-commerce stores to digital services and subscription-based models, the diversity of online business models continues to expand, catering to varied consumer needs.

3. Data-Driven Decision Making: Advanced analytics and data-driven insights empower businesses to understand consumer behaviour, personalize experiences, and make informed strategic decisions.

4. Entrepreneurial Opportunities: The low entry barriers and the abundance of online tools provide aspiring entrepreneurs with unprecedented opportunities to start and scale their ventures.

Advantages of Online Business

Global Reach: Breaking Down Geographical Barriers

One of the paramount advantages that online businesses enjoy is the ability to transcend geographical limitations and reach a global audience. In the realm of traditional brick-and-mortar businesses, expansion beyond local or national borders often involved significant logistical and financial challenges. However, with the advent of online business, these barriers have been dismantled, paving the way for unprecedented opportunities.

The Power of Global Connectivity

1. Access to Diverse Markets: Online platforms provide businesses with the capability to showcase their products or services to a vast and diverse global audience. This opens doors to new markets, untapped consumer segments, and unique cultural landscapes.

2. Efficient Market Entry: Establishing a physical presence in a foreign market requires substantial resources and time. In contrast, online businesses can enter new markets swiftly and cost-effectively, allowing for agile adaptation to changing market dynamics.

Strategies for Maximizing Global Reach

1. Optimized Website and E-Commerce Platforms:

   o Ensure your website and e-commerce platforms are optimized for a global audience, with multilingual options, currency conversions, and international shipping capabilities.

2. Localized Marketing Strategies:

   o Tailor your marketing strategies to resonate with the cultural nuances of different regions. This includes adapting content, imagery, and promotional campaigns to suit the preferences of diverse audiences.

3. Utilizing Global Marketplaces:

   o Leverage international e-commerce platforms and marketplaces to expand your reach. Platforms like Amazon, eBay, and Alibaba provide access to a vast customer base around the world.

Case Study: The Global Success of Alibaba

In the dynamic landscape of e-commerce, few stories captivate the imagination quite like that of Alibaba Group. What began as a visionary endeavour in a Hangzhou apartment has evolved into a global juggernaut, reshaping the way business is conducted and illustrating the unparalleled power of global reach in the digital age.

Background
- Founder: Jack Ma
- Founding Year: 1999
- Headquarters: Hangzhou, China

The Alibaba Vision

Jack Ma's vision for Alibaba was ambitious yet simple — to create a platform that would connect small and medium-sized enterprises (SMEs) with customers globally. Alibaba's initial focus on the Chinese market quickly expanded, leading to the creation of Alibaba.com, a global online marketplace facilitating trade between businesses worldwide.
Advantages of Global Reach for Alibaba

1. *Market Access for SMEs:*

   o Alibaba's global reach provided a gateway for countless small businesses, enabling them to showcase their products to a vast international audience. This inclusive approach empowered SMEs to compete on a global scale.

2. *Cross-Border Trade Facilitation:*

   o Alibaba's platforms, including Alibaba.com and AliExpress, simplified cross-border trade by providing secure payment gateways, logistics support, and a trusted framework for international transactions.

3. *Cultural Adaptation:*

   o Alibaba's success in diverse markets can be attributed to its adeptness at adapting its platforms to suit local cultural nuances. From language options to culturally relevant marketing strategies, Alibaba personalized its approach for each region.

4. *Expansion into Diverse Business Sectors:*

   o Beyond e-commerce, Alibaba expanded its reach into various sectors, including cloud computing, digital entertainment, and financial services, creating a diversified ecosystem that resonated globally.

Strategies Employed by Alibaba

1. E-commerce Dominance:

   o Alibaba's e-commerce platforms, such as Taobao and Tmall, became household names, offering an extensive array of products and services.

2. Global Marketplaces:

   o Alibaba strategically entered global marketplaces, connecting international buyers and sellers. AliExpress, for instance, became a go-to platform for consumers seeking unique products directly from overseas sellers.

3. Investment in Technology:

   o Alibaba's commitment to technological innovation, including advancements in artificial intelligence and cloud computing, solidified its position as a technological powerhouse.

Navigating Challenges

1. Regulatory Compliance:

   o Alibaba navigated complex international regulations by establishing localized operations and collaborating with local authorities to ensure compliance.
2. Logistical Efficiency:

   o Addressing logistical challenges, Alibaba invested in state-of-the-art logistics infrastructure, including the development of Caimito, its logistics platform.
   o Impact on Global E-Commerce

Alibaba's journey serves as an inspiration for businesses aspiring to harness the advantages of global reach. Its success underscores the transformative potential of breaking down geographical barriers, fostering cross-cultural connections, and creating an inclusive global marketplace.
As we explore the advantages of online business further, let Alibaba's story be a testament to the boundless possibilities that await those who dare to dream on a global scale.

The Economic Advantage of Online Business

The concept of cost-efficiency holds paramount importance. Online businesses, by their very nature, offer a distinct economic advantage over traditional brick-and-mortar models. Let's explore how the digital landscape facilitates cost-effectiveness and operational efficiency. Reduced Overheads and Operational Costs.

1. *No Physical Storefronts:*

   o Traditional businesses often bear the burden of high rental costs for prime physical locations. In contrast, online businesses eliminate the need for brick-and-mortar storefronts, reducing significant overhead costs.

2. *Inventory Management:*

   o Online businesses can adopt lean inventory management practices, minimizing the need for extensive storage spaces and reducing carrying costs associated with excess stock.

Streamlined Operations and Automation

1. *Automated Processes:*

   o Automation is a hallmark of online businesses, streamlining various operational processes. Tasks such as order processing, inventory tracking, and customer support can be automated, reducing the need for extensive manpower.

2. *Digital Marketing vs. Traditional Advertising:*

   o Online businesses leverage digital marketing channels, which often prove more cost-effective than traditional advertising. Social media, content marketing, and email campaigns offer targeted reach at a fraction of the cost of traditional advertising methods.

Global Sourcing and Outsourcing

1. *Global Sourcing of Goods and Services:*

   o Online businesses can explore global markets for sourcing products and services, allowing them to find cost-effective solutions and negotiate favourable terms with suppliers.

2. *Outsourcing Non-Core Functions:*

   o Outsourcing non-core functions such as customer support, logistics, and IT services can significantly reduce operational costs. Online businesses can tap into a global pool of talent for specialized tasks.

Data-Driven Decision Making

1. *Analytics for Efficiency:*

   o The availability of advanced analytics tools allows online businesses to make data-driven decisions. This enhances operational efficiency by identifying cost-saving opportunities, optimizing processes, and understanding customer behaviours.

Case Study: Amazon and Operational Efficiency

Amazon, founded by Jeff Bezos in 1994, stands as a testament to the transformative power of operational efficiency in the world of e-commerce. From its humble beginnings as an online bookstore to its current status as a global e-commerce and technology giant, Amazon's success is deeply rooted in its relentless pursuit of operational excellence.

Operational Efficiency Strategies

1. *Lean Supply Chain Management:*

   o Amazon has pioneered a lean and efficient supply chain, utilizing advanced logistics technologies and an extensive network of fulfilment centres to reduce delivery times and costs.

2. *Automated Warehousing:*

   o Amazon's fulfilment centres are equipped with state-of-the-art robotics and automation, optimizing order fulfilment processes and minimizing labour costs.

3. *Dynamic Pricing Models:*

   o Amazon employs dynamic pricing algorithms, adjusting product prices based on real-time market demand, competitor pricing, and other factors. This ensures competitive pricing while maximizing profitability.

4. *Customer-Centric Technology:*

   o Investments in customer-centric technologies, such as the Amazon Prime loyalty program and the use of artificial intelligence for personalized recommendations, enhance customer satisfaction and drive repeat business.

Global Sourcing and Marketplace:

1. *Diverse Product Sourcing:*

   o Amazon's marketplace model allows it to source a vast array of products from sellers worldwide, optimizing costs by tapping into a global supply chain.

2. *Fulfilment by Amazon (FBA):*

   o FBA enables third-party sellers to leverage Amazon's logistics infrastructure, reducing the operational burden on sellers and ensuring swift, cost-effective order fulfilment.

Data-Driven Decision Making:

1. Advanced Analytics:
   o Amazon relies heavily on data analytics to make informed decisions. From predicting consumer preferences to optimizing inventory levels, data-driven insights play a pivotal role in Amazon's operational efficiency.

2. Continuous Improvement Culture:
   o Amazon follows a culture of continuous improvement, constantly iterating on its processes based on data feedback. This commitment to innovation ensures that the company remains at the forefront of operational efficiency.

Challenges and Solutions:

1. Logistical Complexity:
   o Amazon has addressed the logistical complexity of global operations through strategic investments in transportation and last-mile delivery solutions, ensuring efficient order fulfilment.
2. Workforce Management:
   o Amazon's emphasis on employee training, engagement, and well-being addresses workforce challenges, fostering a culture of efficiency and productivity.

Impact on Cost-Efficiency:

Amazon's relentless pursuit of operational efficiency has translated into cost-effectiveness across its operations. The ability to offer competitive prices, expedited delivery options, and a vast product selection has contributed to Amazon's dominance in the global e-commerce landscape.

Key Takeaways for Online Businesses:

1. Invest in Technology:

   o Embrace technological solutions that enhance efficiency, automate processes, and provide valuable insights into customer behaviour.

2. Global Marketplace Dynamics:

   o Explore the benefits of a global marketplace model, tapping into diverse sourcing options and leveraging a worldwide customer base.

3. Customer-Centric Approach:

   o Prioritize customer satisfaction through personalized experiences, efficient logistics, and value-added services.

As we explore the advantages of online business, Amazon's case study serves as a compelling illustration of how operational efficiency can be a game-changer in the highly competitive digital landscape.

Navigating Challenges: Balancing Cost-Efficiency and Quality
While the cost-efficiency of online businesses is undeniable, maintaining quality and customer satisfaction remains paramount. Striking the right balance between cost savings and delivering value is crucial for sustained success.
As we continue our exploration of the advantages of online business, let's unravel how digital platforms empower entrepreneurs to operate leaner, smarter, and more cost-effectively in the competitive global marketplace.

Operating 24/7 in the Digital Age

In the realm of online business, the concept of time transcends traditional constraints. The ability to operate 24/7 stands as a hallmark of digital flexibility, offering unparalleled convenience for both businesses and customers.

Advantages for Online Businesses

1. *Continuous Revenue Generation:*

   o Operating round the clock means that your online storefront is always open for business. This continuous availability allows for ongoing revenue generation, irrespective of time zones or geographical locations.

2. *Global Engagement:*

   o Online businesses have the capability to engage with a global audience at any hour. Whether it's daytime in one part of the world or night time in another, your products or services are accessible to potential customers, expanding your reach beyond local constraints.

3. *Real-Time Adaptability:*

   o The digital landscape facilitates real-time adaptability. Online businesses can respond swiftly to market changes, consumer demands, and emerging trends, adjusting their offerings and strategies without the limitations of traditional business hours.

Customer-Centric Convenience

1. *24/7 Shopping Convenience:*

   o Customers appreciate the convenience of being able to browse, shop, and make transactions at any time that suits their schedule. This flexibility is particularly advantageous for individuals with busy lifestyles or those in different time zones.

2. *Instant Access to Information:*

   o The availability of information and customer support at all hours enhances the overall shopping experience. Customers can access product details, reviews, and assistance whenever they need it, contributing to a seamless and satisfying online journey.

3. *Flexible Communication Channels:*

   o Online businesses can leverage various communication channels, including live chat, chatbots, and email support, to maintain communication with customers 24/7. This accessibility builds trust and loyalty.

Disadvantages and Challenges
Navigating the Crowded Online Space

The online business is teeming with opportunities, but it comes with its share of challenges, chief among them being heightened competition. In this section, we'll explore the dynamics of online competition and strategies for standing out in a crowded digital marketplace.

Understanding Online Competition

1. *Saturation in Market Niches:*

   o Many market niches are saturated with businesses offering similar products or services. Standing out requires a unique value proposition and strategic differentiation.

2. *Global Reach and Diverse Competitors:*

   o The global nature of online business means that competitors can emerge from any corner of the world. Understanding and staying ahead of diverse competitors is crucial.

Strategies to Stand Out

1. *Unique Value Proposition (UVP):*

   o Clearly define your UVP to communicate what sets your business apart. Whether it's exceptional quality, personalized services, or innovative solutions, a strong UVP resonates with customers.

2. *Niche Targeting:*

   o Identify and target specific niches within your industry. Tailoring your products or services to meet the unique needs of a niche audience can lead to more impactful and focused marketing.

3. *Exceptional Customer Experience:*

   o Prioritize customer experience to build loyalty and positive word-of-mouth. From seamless website navigation to responsive customer support, every interaction contributes to the overall experience.

4. *Innovative Marketing Strategies:*

   o Embrace innovative marketing strategies, such as influencer collaborations, interactive content, and experiential campaigns, to capture and retain the attention of your target audience.

5. *Data-Driven Marketing:*

   o Leverage data analytics to understand customer behavior and preferences. Data-driven insights enable targeted marketing efforts, optimizing your promotional strategies for maximum impact.

Case Study:

E-commerce Business and Successful Differentiation
Include a brief case study highlighting a specific e-commerce business that successfully navigated competition, detailing the strategies implemented, and the resulting impact on market positioning.
Navigating Challenges: Building Resilience in Competitive Spaces
Overcoming the challenges of competition requires ongoing adaptation and resilience. Stay attuned to industry trends, monitor competitor activities, and be willing to evolve your strategies to maintain a competitive edge.

Staying Ahead in a Dynamic Digital Landscape

The digital landscape is marked by rapid technological advancements, presenting businesses with both opportunities and technical challenges. In this section, we'll explore potential technical issues and underscore the importance of staying updated on technology trends.
Potential Technical Challenges.

1. *Cybersecurity Threats:*

   o Online businesses are susceptible to cybersecurity threats, including data breaches and cyberattacks. Ensuring robust cybersecurity measures is essential to protect sensitive information.

2. *Website Performance Issues:*

   o Technical glitches, slow loading times, and website downtime can significantly impact the user experience. Regular website audits and optimization.

3. *Compatibility Across Devices:*

   o Challenge: With users accessing websites from various devices and browsers, ensuring compatibility is a complex challenge.
   o Strategy: Adopt responsive design principles, conduct cross-browser testing, and prioritize mobile optimization. Regularly update design practices to accommodate new devices and screen sizes.

4. *Data Privacy and Compliance:*

- o Challenge: Evolving data protection regulations and consumer privacy concerns require businesses to navigate a complex landscape of compliance.
- o Strategy: Stay abreast of data protection laws, such as GDPR and CCPA, and ensure that your business practices align with these regulations. Implement transparent data collection policies and obtain explicit consent from users.

5. *Technological Obsolescence:*

- o Challenge: Rapid advancements in technology can render existing systems obsolete, impacting performance and competitiveness.
- o Strategy: Foster a culture of innovation within the organization. Regularly assess the technological landscape, invest in ongoing education for the team, and plan for timely upgrades to prevent obsolescence.

6. *Scalability Challenges:*

- o Challenge: Sudden surges in website traffic or business growth can strain existing infrastructure, leading to scalability challenges.
- o Strategy: Design systems with scalability in mind, utilize cloud-based services for flexible resource allocation, and conduct stress testing to identify potential bottlenecks. Plan for scalability as an integral part of the business strategy.

Navigating Technical Challenges: A Proactive Approach

Successfully navigating technical challenges requires a proactive approach that combines vigilant monitoring, strategic planning, and a commitment to ongoing learning. Embrace a culture of adaptability and resilience to thrive in the dynamic digital landscape.

In the upcoming sections, we'll delve deeper into strategies and best practices for overcoming these challenges, ensuring that your online business not only survives but thrives in the face of technical complexities.

Chapter 2: Finding Your Niche
How to Identify a Profitable Niche

Embarking on the journey of building a successful online business starts with the crucial step of identifying a profitable niche. This process involves a delicate balance between personal passion, market demand, and strategic evaluation. Here's a comprehensive guide to help you pinpoint a niche that aligns with your goals and has the potential for success.

- **Personal Passion and Skills**: Your journey begins with self-reflection. What are you truly passionate about, and what skills do you possess? Your business is not merely a venture; it's an extension of your interests and expertise. When passion meets skill, the foundation for a thriving business is laid.

- **Market Demand Analysis**: Dive into the digital landscape to gauge market demand. Utilize online tools, forums, and social media platforms to identify trending topics and products. Assess their popularity and the conversations surrounding them. A niche with a substantial demand base provides a fertile ground for your business to flourish.

- **Keyword Research**: Navigate the digital terrain through keyword research. Explore search terms related to your interests and potential niches. Analyse search volumes and competition levels. Keywords act as signposts, guiding you toward topics that resonate with online audiences.

- **Problem Solving**: Great businesses often arise from addressing specific problems or pain points. Look within your areas of interest for challenges that people are facing. A niche that offers solutions to real problems becomes not just a business but a valuable resource for your audience.

- **Audience Validation**: Before committing to a niche, seek validation from your potential audience. Conduct surveys, host focus groups, or create a small Minimum Viable Product (MVP) to gather feedback. Understanding the needs and preferences of your target audience is paramount.

- **Profitability Assessment**: While passion is a driving force, profitability sustains a business. Evaluate the potential profitability of your chosen niche. Consider the average transaction value, potential for repeat business, and the overall size of the market. A profitable niche ensures the longevity of your venture.

Conducting Market Research and Competitor Analysis

Once you've identified a potential niche, the next crucial step is to understand the market landscape and analyse your competitors. This in-depth research sets the stage for strategic positioning and differentiation.

1. Define Your Target Audience: Clarity about your target audience is foundational. Clearly define demographics, preferences, behaviours, and challenges. This information shapes your marketing strategy and ensures that your offerings resonate with your intended audience.
2. Competitor Identification: Identify key players in your chosen niche. Analyse their products, pricing, and marketing strategies. This step unveils valuable insights into the existing market dynamics and helps you identify opportunities for innovation.

- SWOT Analysis: A SWOT analysis is a powerful tool to assess both your business and your competitors. Evaluate Strengths, Weaknesses, Opportunities, and Threats. This analysis guides strategic decision-making and highlights areas where you can excel.

- Customer Feedback Analysis: Delve into customer feedback regarding competitors' products or services. Understand common pain points, areas of satisfaction, and any unmet needs. This analysis serves as a compass for refining your own offerings.

- Unique Selling Proposition (USP): Craft a Unique Selling Proposition (USP) that sets your business apart. Clearly communicate what makes your offerings superior or distinctive. A compelling USP is the cornerstone of effective branding and customer acquisition.

- Market Trends and Dynamics: The digital landscape is dynamic, and staying abreast of market trends is vital. Regularly monitor industry publications, blogs, and social media channels to understand shifts, emerging opportunities, and potential threats. Adaptability is a key driver of long-term success.

Conclusion
Congratulations on navigating the intricate process of finding your niche and conducting comprehensive market research. These steps lay the groundwork for a resilient and informed approach to your online business journey. As you conclude Chapter 2, reflect on the valuable insights gained and the strategic decisions ahead. In Chapter 3, we will delve into transforming your niche into a compelling online presence. Your entrepreneurial journey is gaining momentum—keep moving forward with confidence!

Chapter 3: Building Your Online Presence
Creating a Professional Website

Your online presence begins with a virtual storefront—the embodiment of your brand and offerings. Crafting a professional website is more than a technical task; it's an art that blends design, functionality, and user experience. Let's delve into the key aspects of creating a website that not only showcases your business but also captivates your audience.

- Define Your Brand Identity: Building a website starts with a clear understanding of your brand identity. What values and principles does your business embody? Reflect these in your website's design, color scheme, and messaging. Consistency in branding builds trust.

- Choose an Intuitive Domain Name: Your domain name is your online address. Select a domain name that is easy to remember, relevant to your business, and aligns with your brand. Ensure it is unique and reflects the essence of your niche.

- User-Friendly Design: User experience is paramount. Design your website with the user in mind—intuitive navigation, clear calls-to-action, and visually appealing layouts. A user-friendly design encourages exploration and engagement.

- Mobile Responsiveness: The rise of mobile users mandates a mobile-responsive design. Ensure that your website is optimized for various devices, providing a seamless experience for users whether they're on desktops, tablets, or smartphones.

- Compelling Content: Content is the heartbeat of your website. Craft compelling, informative content that communicates your products or services, unique value proposition, and brand story. High-quality content not only engages visitors but also establishes your authority in the industry.

- Implement SEO Best Practices: Optimize your website for search engines. Incorporate relevant keywords, optimize meta tags, and focus on providing valuable content. Effective SEO practices enhance your website's visibility, driving organic traffic.

- Secure Your Website: Security is non-negotiable. Implement SSL certificates, secure payment gateways, and conduct regular security audits. A secure website not only protects sensitive information but also instills confidence in your customers.

  8. A.I. Integration: Consider the integration of Artificial Intelligence (A.I.) to elevate your website's functionality. A.I.-powered chatbots can provide real-time customer support, enhancing user experience. Explore A.I. analytics for valuable insights into user behaviour.

Utilizing social media and Other Online Platforms

Social media and online platforms are dynamic arenas for engagement and brand visibility. Effectively leveraging these channels requires a thoughtful strategy that aligns with your business goals. Let's explore how to strategically utilize social media and other online platforms to amplify your online presence.

- Choose Relevant Social Media Channels: Identify the social media platforms most frequented by your target audience. Each platform caters to distinct demographics. Choose wisely to focus your efforts where your audience is most active.

- Develop a Content Calendar: Consistency is key in the realm of social media. Plan and schedule your content using a content calendar. This not only ensures regular engagement but also allows you to align your posts with broader marketing strategies.

- Engage with Your Audience: social media is a two-way street. Actively engage with your audience through comments, direct messages, and polls. Respond promptly, encourage discussions, and build a community around your brand. Engaged followers are loyal followers.

- Utilize Visual Content: Visual content is a potent tool for storytelling. Leverage high-quality images, infographics, and videos to capture attention and convey your brand story. Visuals leave a lasting impression and enhance engagement.

- Leverage Online Platforms: Beyond social media, explore additional online platforms relevant to your business. Consider e-commerce marketplaces, review sites, or industry-specific forums. Diversifying your online presence extends your reach and taps into different audience segments.

- Incorporating A.I. for Enhanced Online Presence: Artificial Intelligence (A.I.) can be a game-changer in bolstering your online presence. A.I.-driven chatbots provide instant responses to customer queries, improving user experience. Explore personalized content recommendations based on A.I. analytics to enhance engagement.

- Monitor Analytics and Adjust: Regularly monitor analytics on your website and social media platforms. Analyse user behaviour, track Key Performance Indicators (KPIs), and use insights to refine your online strategy. Adaptability is a key driver of success in the dynamic digital landscape.

- Utilize Email Marketing: Email marketing remains a potent tool for customer engagement. Build an email list and craft targeted campaigns. Personalized and relevant emails can drive traffic to your website and nurture customer relationships.

Conclusion

As we conclude this Chapter, you've explored the intricacies of creating a professional website, strategically utilizing social media and online platforms, and integrating Artificial Intelligence to enhance your online presence. The digital landscape is vast, and your effective navigation through it positions your business for success. In the next Chapter, we'll delve into proven online marketing strategies to drive traffic and conversions. Keep the momentum going, and let your online presence shine!

Chapter 4: E-Commerce Essentials
Setting Up an Online Store

Entering the realm of e-commerce is a transformative step for your business. Setting up an online store involves more than just listing products—it's about creating a seamless and engaging platform for customers to explore, choose, and purchase. Let's delve into the essentials of establishing a robust online store.

- *Choose the Right E-Commerce Platform:*
  Selecting the right e-commerce platform is foundational. Options like Shopify, WooCommerce, and BigCommerce offer varying features and scalability. Consider your business needs, budget, and technical requirements when making this crucial decision.

- *Design a User-Friendly Interface:*
  Your online store's design should prioritize user experience. Ensure intuitive navigation, clear product categorization, and compelling visuals. The goal is to guide visitors seamlessly through their shopping journey.

- *Product Listings and Descriptions:*
  Craft detailed and engaging product listings. Include high-quality images, comprehensive descriptions, and any relevant specifications. Transparency in product information builds trust with your customers.

- *Implement a Responsive Design:*
  Mobile responsiveness is non-negotiable. A significant portion of online shopping happens on mobile devices. Optimize your store for various screen sizes to ensure a consistent and enjoyable experience.

- *Streamline the Checkout Process:*
  Simplify the checkout process to reduce friction for customers. Minimize the number of steps, offer guest checkout options, and provide multiple payment methods. A seamless checkout experience encourages completed transactions.

- *Integrate Inventory Management:*
  Efficient inventory management is critical. Integrate systems that track stock levels, automatically update product availability, and provide alerts for low stock. Preventing overselling enhances customer satisfaction.

- *Provide Customer Support:*
  Offer accessible customer support options, such as live chat, email, or a dedicated helpline. Promptly address customer queries and concerns to build trust and loyalty.

- *Utilize A.I. for Personalization:*
  Leverage Artificial Intelligence (A.I.) to personalize the shopping experience. Implement recommendation engines that suggest products based on customer preferences, purchase history, and browsing behaviour.

Payment Gateways, Security, and Customer Trust

Ensuring secure transactions and building customer trust are paramount in the world of e-commerce. Explore the intricacies of payment gateways, security measures, and strategies to instil confidence in your customers.

- *Choose Reliable Payment Gateways:*
  Select reputable and secure payment gateways to process transactions. Popular options include PayPal, Stripe, and Square. Provide a variety of payment options to accommodate diverse customer preferences.

- *Prioritize Security Measures:*
  Security is non-negotiable in e-commerce. Implement SSL certificates to secure data transmission, use secure and encrypted payment gateways, and regularly update your website's security protocols. Customer trust hinges on the safety of their information.
- *Display Trust Seals and Reviews:*
  Display trust seals, such as SSL certifications and security badges, prominently on your website. Additionally, showcase customer reviews and testimonials to build credibility. Positive social proof enhances customer confidence.
- *Transparent Policies and Communication:*
  Clearly communicate your business policies, including shipping, returns, and privacy. Transparency fosters trust, and customers are more likely to make purchases when they understand your commitment to their satisfaction.

- *Implement Two-Factor Authentication:*
  Enhance account security by implementing two-factor authentication (2FA). This additional layer of protection adds an extra barrier against unauthorized access, safeguarding customer accounts.
- *Regular Security Audits:*
  Conduct regular security audits to identify vulnerabilities and proactively address potential threats. Stay informed about the latest security best practices and updates to protect your e-commerce platform.
- *Provide Order Tracking:*
  Offer order tracking functionality to keep customers informed about the status of their purchases. Real-time updates instil confidence and reduce uncertainty, contributing to a positive post-purchase experience.
- *Utilize A.I. for Fraud Detection:*
  Leverage A.I. algorithms for fraud detection. A.I.-powered systems can analyse patterns and anomalies in transactions, helping identify and prevent fraudulent activities.

Conclusion

Congratulations on navigating the essentials of e-commerce. In this chapter, we've explored the intricacies of setting up an online store, optimizing the user experience, and ensuring secure transactions. As you continue your e-commerce journey, focus on building a platform that not only facilitates transactions but also cultivates trust and loyalty. In Chapter 5, we will delve into effective online marketing strategies to drive traffic, enhance visibility, and boost sales. Keep the momentum going, and let your e-commerce venture thrive!

Chapter 5: Digital Marketing Strategies
Overview of SEO, Social Media Marketing, and Email Marketing

Embarking on effective digital marketing strategies is essential to amplify your online presence, drive traffic, and foster customer engagement. In this chapter, we will delve into the foundational aspects of SEO, social media marketing, and email marketing.

Search Engine Optimization (SEO):

Search Engine Optimization (SEO) is the cornerstone of online visibility. It involves optimizing your website to rank higher on search engine results pages, making it easier for potential customers to find your business.

Key Components of SEO:

1. *Keyword Research:*
   - Identify relevant keywords related to your business. Utilize tools like Google Keyword Planner to discover high-value keywords with decent search volumes.
2. *On-Page Optimization:*
   - Optimize meta titles, meta descriptions, and heading tags on your website. Ensure that your content is structured, easy to read, and incorporates targeted keywords.

3. *Quality Content:*
    - Develop high-quality, relevant, and informative content. Regularly update your blog and create content that resonates with your target audience.
4. *Link Building:*
    - Build a strong backlink profile by acquiring high-quality inbound links. Collaborate with influencers, guest post on reputable websites, and foster relationships within your industry.

5. *Mobile Optimization:*
    - Ensure your website is optimized for mobile devices. Google prioritizes mobile-friendly websites in its rankings, making this an essential aspect of SEO.

Social Media Marketing:

Social media is a dynamic channel for brand promotion, customer engagement, and community building. Understanding the nuances of each platform and tailoring your strategy accordingly is crucial. Key Components of Social Media Marketing:

1. *Platform Selection:*
    - Identify social media platforms where your target audience is most active. Platforms like Facebook, Instagram, Twitter, LinkedIn, and Pinterest cater to different demographics.
2. *Content Calendar:*
    - Develop a content calendar outlining your posting schedule. Consistency is vital for maintaining audience engagement. Plan posts that align with your overall marketing strategy.
3. *Visual Content:*
    - Leverage the power of visual content. Use high-quality images, infographics, and videos to capture attention and convey your brand message effectively.
4. *Engagement Strategies:*
    - Actively engage with your audience through comments, direct messages, and polls. Encourage user-generated content, run contests, and foster a sense of community around your brand.

Email Marketing:

Email marketing remains a potent tool for direct communication with your audience. Crafting personalized and relevant email campaigns can drive traffic, nurture leads, and boost sales.
Key Components of Email Marketing:

1. *Build an Email List:*
   o Develop strategies to build a subscriber list. Offer incentives such as exclusive discounts, downloadable content, or newsletters to encourage sign-ups.

2. *Segmentation:*
   o Segment your email list based on demographics, preferences, and behaviours. Targeted and personalized emails have a higher chance of resonating with specific audience segments.
3. *Compelling Content:*
   o Craft compelling email content that aligns with your audience's interests and needs. Use persuasive copy, enticing visuals, and clear calls-to-action.
4. *Automation:*
   o Implement automation for email campaigns. Set up automated workflows for welcome emails, abandoned cart reminders, and post-purchase follow-ups to streamline your communication.

Creating a Content Marketing Plan

Content marketing is the backbone of your digital presence, providing value to your audience while strategically promoting your brand. Crafting a comprehensive content marketing plan involves careful planning, diverse content formats, and consistent delivery.

Key Components of a Content Marketing Plan:

1. *Define Goals and Objectives:*

   o Clearly outline your content marketing goals. Whether it's increasing brand awareness, driving traffic, or boosting sales, align your content strategy with your overall business objectives.

2. *Audience Persona Development:*

   o Understand your target audience's demographics, preferences, and pain points. Create audience personas to guide your content creation process and ensure relevance.

3. *Content Calendar:*

   o Develop a content calendar that outlines your content creation and publication schedule. Plan content themes, topics, and formats to maintain consistency and relevance.

4. *Diverse Content Formats:*

   o Experiment with various content formats such as blog posts, infographics, videos, podcasts, and interactive content. Diversifying formats keeps your content strategy engaging and caters to different audience preferences.

5. *Keyword Integration:*

   o Integrate relevant keywords naturally into your content. This not only aligns with SEO best practices but also ensures your content is discoverable by your target audience.

6. *Promotion Strategies:*

   o Plan how you will promote your content. Utilize social media, email newsletters, influencer partnerships, and other channels to maximize the reach of your valuable content.

7. *Measure and Analyse:*

   o Implement analytics tools to track the performance of your content. Measure metrics such as engagement, conversion rates, and audience growth. Analyse data to refine your content strategy continually.

Conclusion

Congratulations on exploring the foundational elements of digital marketing strategies. In this chapter, we've covered the essentials of SEO, social media marketing, email marketing, and creating a content marketing plan. As you move forward, remember that digital marketing is a dynamic landscape, requiring adaptability and continuous refinement of strategies. In the next Chapter, we will delve into the realm of data analytics and how it can enhance your decision-making processes. Keep the momentum going, and let your digital marketing efforts propel your business to new heights!

Chapter 6: Effective Product and Service Offerings

Developing and Pricing Products/Services

Creating and pricing your products or services involves a delicate balance between meeting customer needs, maintaining profitability, and staying competitive in the market. In this chapter, we will explore the strategic considerations for developing and pricing offerings that resonate with your target audience.

Developing Products/Services:

1. *Market Research:*

   o Begin with comprehensive market research to understand current trends, customer preferences, and gaps in the market. Identify opportunities for innovation and areas where your offerings can stand out.

2. *Customer Feedback:*

   o Actively seek and incorporate customer feedback in the product development process. Understand the pain points and desires of your target audience to tailor your offerings accordingly.

3. *Quality and Differentiation:*

   o Emphasize quality in your products or services. Consider how you can differentiate your offerings from competitors, whether through unique features, superior performance, or exceptional customer service.

4. *Scalability:*

   o Evaluate the scalability of your offerings. Consider future growth and expansion, and design products or services that can adapt to changing market dynamics and increasing demand.

5. *Testing and Iteration:*

   o Conduct pilot tests or prototype launches to gather real-world feedback before a full-scale launch. Use this information to iterate and refine your offerings, ensuring they meet or exceed customer expectations.

Pricing Strategy:

1. *Cost-Based Pricing:*

   o Calculate the cost of production, distribution, and any other associated expenses. Add a reasonable profit margin to determine the baseline price. This approach ensures you cover costs and generate profit.

2. *Value-Based Pricing:*

   o Set prices based on the perceived value of your offerings to the customer. Consider factors such as quality, brand reputation, and unique features. This strategy allows for higher pricing if your product or service provides significant value.

3. *Competitive Pricing:*

   o Analyse the pricing strategies of competitors in your industry. Set your prices in alignment with market standards while considering factors that make your offerings distinctive.

4. *Dynamic Pricing:*

   o Implement dynamic pricing strategies that respond to market conditions, demand fluctuations, and other variables. This approach allows for flexibility and responsiveness to changes in the business environment.

5. *Bundling and Upselling:*

   o Explore bundling options or upselling complementary products or services. This strategy can enhance the perceived value for customers and increase overall revenue.

Understanding Customer Needs and Demands

Understanding your customers is foundational to delivering offerings that not only meet but exceed their expectations. In this section, we will explore methods for gaining insights into customer needs and demands.

Customer Surveys and Feedback:

1. *Regular Surveys:*

   o Conduct regular customer surveys to gather feedback on your existing products or services. Ask about satisfaction levels, areas for improvement, and any additional features they desire.

2. *Feedback Forms:*

   o Implement feedback forms on your website, during the checkout process, or through post-purchase emails. Encourage customers to share their experiences and suggestions for enhancing your offerings.

3. *Social Media Listening:*

   o Monitor social media channels for mentions of your brand, products, or industry-related discussions. Social media platforms can provide valuable insights into customer sentiments and emerging trends.

Data Analytics:

1. *Website Analytics:*

   o Utilize website analytics tools to track user behaviour on your online platforms. Analyse which products or services attract the most attention, how customers navigate your site, and where they drop off.

2. *Purchase History Analysis:*

   o Analyse customer purchase histories to identify patterns and preferences. Understand which products or services are frequently purchased together, enabling strategic bundling or cross-selling opportunities.

3. *Customer Segmentation:*

   o Implement customer segmentation based on demographics, behaviours, or purchase history. Tailor marketing messages and offerings to different segments, providing a personalized experience.

Direct Customer Interaction:

1. *Customer Support Channels:*

   o Leverage customer support channels for direct interaction. Encourage customers to reach out with questions or concerns, and use these interactions to gain deeper insights into their needs and expectations.

2. *Focus Groups:*

   o Conduct focus group sessions with select customers to delve into their experiences and preferences. These sessions provide qualitative insights and allow for in-depth discussions.

3. *Product Trials and Demos:*

   o Offer product trials or demos to allow customers to experience your offerings first hand. Gather feedback during these trials to understand their reactions and expectations.

Conclusion

Congratulations on exploring the intricacies of developing, pricing, and understanding customer needs for your products and services. In this chapter, we've addressed the crucial considerations for creating offerings that align with customer expectations and market dynamics. In the next Chapter, we will delve into effective sales strategies and customer relationship management to drive revenue and foster long-term loyalty. Keep the momentum going, and let your offerings become a cornerstone of success in your business journey.

Chapter 7: Building a Brand
Importance of Branding in the Online Space

In the dynamic and competitive online landscape, the significance of branding cannot be overstated. Your brand is more than just a logo or a tagline—it's the perception that customers have about your business. In this chapter, we'll delve into why branding is crucial in the online space and how it forms the foundation for establishing a strong and memorable presence.

Establishing Credibility:

1. *Trust and Credibility:*

   o   A well-defined brand builds trust. In the online realm, where face-to-face interactions are limited, establishing credibility through a consistent and reputable brand is essential for gaining customer trust.

2. *Professionalism:*

   o   A strong brand exudes professionalism. It signals to customers that you take your business seriously, instilling confidence in the quality of your products or services.

3. *Competitive Differentiation:*

    o In a crowded online marketplace, branding sets you apart from competitors. A distinctive brand identity helps customers remember and choose your business over others.

Connecting with the Audience:

1. *Emotional Connection:*

    o Brands that evoke emotions create lasting connections with their audience. Whether through storytelling, values, or a unique brand persona, emotional resonance fosters loyalty.

2. *Targeting the Right Audience:*

    o Effective branding ensures that your messaging resonates with your target audience. It helps you speak directly to the people who are most likely to engage with and benefit from your offerings.

3. *Brand Personality:*

    o Infusing a personality into your brand makes it relatable. Whether it's humour, sincerity, or innovation, a defined personality strengthens the bond between your brand and its audience.

Creating a Consistent Brand Image

Consistency is key when it comes to branding. A consistent brand image across various touchpoints reinforces your identity and leaves a lasting impression on customers. Let's explore how to create and maintain this consistency.

Branding Elements:

1. *Visual Identity:*

    o Your logo, colour palette, typography, and imagery form the visual elements of your brand. Maintain consistency across all platforms to create a cohesive and recognizable look.

2. *Brand Messaging:*

   o Develop a clear and consistent voice for your brand. Whether it's through website copy, social media posts, or marketing materials, a unified message strengthens your brand identity.

3. *Brand Guidelines:*

   o Establish comprehensive brand guidelines outlining the proper use of your branding elements. Share these guidelines with your team to ensure consistency in external communications.

Online Presence:

1. *Website Design:*

   o Your website is a central hub for your online presence. Ensure that its design aligns with your brand identity, creating a seamless and immersive experience for visitors.

2. *Social Media Consistency:*

   o Maintain a cohesive presence across social media platforms. Use consistent profile pictures, cover photos, and messaging to reinforce your brand image.

3. *Email Marketing:*

   o Apply your brand elements to email marketing campaigns. Consistent visuals and messaging in emails contribute to a unified brand experience.

A.I. and Brand Building

Artificial Intelligence (A.I.) plays a transformative role in brand building, offering tools and capabilities that can enhance various aspects of your branding strategy.

A.I.-Driven Personalization:

1. *Personalized Customer Experiences:*

- A.I. algorithms analyse customer data to deliver personalized experiences. Whether through personalized recommendations or targeted content, A.I. enhances customer engagement.

2. *Behavioural Analysis:*

- A.I. tools can analyse customer behaviour on your website and other digital platforms. This data-driven insight helps tailor your brand's messaging and offerings to align with customer preferences.

Chatbots and Virtual Assistants:

1. *Real-Time Interactions:*

- A.I.-powered chatbots provide real-time interactions with customers. They can answer queries, provide information, and guide users through the online experience, contributing to a positive brand impression.

2. *Consistent Messaging:*

- Chatbots ensure consistent messaging aligned with your brand. Whether on your website or social media platforms, the tone and information provided remain in line with your brand guidelines.

A.I.-Enhanced Creativity:

1. *Content Creation:*

- A.I. tools can assist in content creation, generating written or visual content that aligns with your brand style. This ensures a continuous flow of relevant and consistent content.

2. *Visual Recognition:*

- A.I. can analyse visual content to identify and maintain consistency in brand imagery. This includes recognizing your logo in user-generated content across social media platforms.

Predictive Analytics:

1. *Anticipating Customer Needs:*

   o A.I. algorithms predict customer needs based on historical data. This anticipatory approach allows your brand to proactively address customer expectations and preferences.

2. *Adaptive Marketing Strategies:*

   o A.I. analytics provide insights into the effectiveness of marketing strategies. Brands can adapt and refine their approaches based on real-time data, optimizing the impact of their campaigns.
   Conclusion

   Congratulations on understanding the importance of branding in the online space, creating a consistent brand image, and exploring how A.I. can contribute to brand building. In this chapter, we've covered the foundational aspects of branding and how it shapes customer perceptions in the digital realm. In the next Chapter, we will explore effective customer relationship management strategies to cultivate lasting connections with your audience. Keep the momentum going, and let your brand be a beacon of trust and distinction in the online world!

Chapter 8: Customer Relationship Management (CRM)

Importance of Customer Service

In the digital age, where choices abound, the importance of exceptional customer service cannot be overstated. This chapter delves into why customer service is a cornerstone of successful businesses and how it contributes to the overall customer experience.

Retention and Loyalty:

1. *Customer Retention:*

   o Stellar customer service is a powerful tool for retaining existing customers. Satisfied customers are more likely to continue doing business with a brand, contributing to long-term success.

2. *Building Loyalty:*

   o Consistent, positive interactions with customers build loyalty. When customers feel valued and supported, they are more likely to choose your brand over competitors.

Reputation Management:

1. *Word of Mouth:*

   o Exceptional customer service generates positive word of mouth. Satisfied customers become brand advocates, sharing their positive experiences with friends, family, and online communities.

2. *Online Reviews:*

   o Online reviews play a significant role in a brand's reputation. Responsive and effective customer service contributes to positive reviews, enhancing the overall perception of your business.

Differentiation in the Market:

1. *Competitive Edge:*

   o Outstanding customer service sets your brand apart. In a competitive market, where products and prices may be similar, excellent service becomes a key differentiator.

2. *Customer Expectations:*

   o Meeting and exceeding customer expectations creates a positive impression. Brands that consistently go above and beyond in their service delivery stand out in the minds of consumers.

Building and Maintaining Customer Relationships

Building and maintaining strong customer relationships go hand in hand with effective customer service. This section explores strategies for cultivating meaningful connections with your customer base.

Personalization:

1. *Understanding Individual Needs:*

   o   Personalized interactions demonstrate a deep understanding of individual customer needs. Utilize data and customer profiles to tailor your communication and offerings.

2. *Customized Experiences:*

   o   Provide customized experiences based on customer preferences. From personalized recommendations to exclusive offers, tailor your interactions to make customers feel valued.

Effective Communication:

1. *Proactive Communication:*

   o   Proactively communicate with customers. Keep them informed about product updates, promotions, and any relevant information. Transparent communication builds trust.

2. *Multi-Channel Presence:*

   o   Be present across various communication channels. Whether through social media, email, live chat, or phone support, offer multiple avenues for customers to reach out and receive assistance.

Customer Feedback and Surveys:

1. *Feedback Mechanisms:*

   o   Establish mechanisms for collecting customer feedback. Regularly seek input on their experiences, satisfaction levels, and areas for improvement.

2. *Acting on Feedback:*

   o   Act on the feedback received. Demonstrate that customer input is valued by making improvements based on their suggestions and addressing identified issues.

Reward and Recognition:

1. *Loyalty Programs:*

   o Implement loyalty programs to reward repeat customers. These programs can include discounts, exclusive access, or points-based systems that incentivize continued engagement.

2. *Acknowledgment and Recognition:*

   o Acknowledge and recognize loyal customers. Publicly celebrate milestones, such as anniversaries or achievements, to make customers feel appreciated.

A.I. in Customer Relationship Management:

1. *Automated Personalization:*

   o A.I. can analyse customer data to automate personalized experiences. From personalized emails to targeted offers, A.I. enhances the efficiency of delivering tailored interactions.

2. *Predictive Analytics:*

   o Leverage A.I. for predictive analytics. Anticipate customer needs and behaviours based on historical data, allowing you to proactively address issues and offer relevant solutions.

3. *Chatbots for Instant Assistance:*

   o A.I.-powered chatbots provide instant assistance, answering common queries and guiding customers through various processes. This improves response times and enhances the overall customer experience.

4. *Data-Driven Insights:*

   o A.I. tools provide data-driven insights into customer behaviours. Use these insights to understand preferences, identify trends, and make informed decisions about your customer relationship strategies.

Conclusion

Congratulations on exploring the vital role of customer service in the success of your business and strategies for building and maintaining strong customer relationships. In the next Chapter, we will delve into the realm of data analytics and how it can be harnessed to inform business decisions and enhance overall efficiency. Keep the momentum going, and let your commitment to exceptional customer relationships be a driving force in your business journey!

Chapter 9: Analytics and Data-Driven Decisions

Web Analytics Tools

In the digital era, leveraging data analytics is pivotal for informed decision-making and optimizing business performance. This chapter provides an introduction to web analytics tools and delves into how data can be harnessed to enhance your business operations.

Web Analytics Overview:

1. *Definition of Web Analytics:*

   o Web analytics involves the collection, measurement, analysis, and reporting of web data to understand and optimize web usage. It provides insights into user behaviour, website performance, and the effectiveness of online strategies.

2. *Key Metrics:*

   o Web analytics tools track various metrics, including website traffic, user engagement, conversion rates, and more. Understanding these metrics helps businesses assess the success of their online initiatives.

Popular Web Analytics Tools:

1. *Google Analytics:*

   o Google Analytics is a widely used web analytics platform. It offers a comprehensive suite of tools to track and analyse website traffic, user behaviour, and conversion data.

2. *Adobe Analytics:*

   o Adobe Analytics provides advanced analytics capabilities, allowing businesses to gain deep insights into customer journeys, segmentation, and online interactions.

3. *Matomo (formerly Piwik):*

   o Matomo is an open-source web analytics platform that provides customizable analytics reports, ensuring data privacy and ownership for users.

4. *Hotjar:*

   o Hotjar combines analytics and user feedback tools. It offers heatmaps, session recordings, and surveys to understand user behaviour and preferences.

Setting Up Web Analytics:

1. *Account Creation:*

   o Create an account on the chosen web analytics platform. For example, sign up for a Google Analytics account and integrate the tracking code into your website.

2. *Defining Goals and Conversions:*

   o Clearly define business goals and conversions that align with your overall objectives. This could include tracking purchases, form submissions, or other user interactions.

3. *Configuring E-commerce Tracking:*

    o   If applicable, configure e-commerce tracking to gain insights into online transactions, revenue, and product performance.

4. *Segmentation and Customization:*

    o   Utilize segmentation and customization features to tailor reports and analyses based on specific criteria, such as user demographics, geography, or device.

Using Data to Improve Business Performance

Harnessing data is a strategic imperative for businesses looking to optimize performance and stay competitive. This section explores how data-driven decisions can positively impact various aspects of your business.

Key Areas of Business Improvement:

1. *Marketing Optimization:*

    o   Analyse marketing data to identify the most effective channels, campaigns, and messaging. Optimize marketing strategies based on data insights to maximize return on investment.

2. *User Experience Enhancement:*

    o   Utilize user behaviour data to enhance the user experience. Identify pain points, optimize navigation, and improve website functionality based on user interactions.

3. *Product and Service Innovation:*

    o   Analyse customer feedback, market trends, and product performance data to drive innovation. Use data to identify opportunities for new products or enhancements to existing offerings.

Business Efficiency and Operations:

1. *Supply Chain Optimization:*

    o Use data to optimize supply chain processes. Analyse demand patterns, inventory levels, and supplier performance to streamline operations and reduce costs.

2. *Financial Performance Monitoring:*

    o Monitor financial data to assess the health of your business. Analyse revenue trends, cost structures, and profitability to make informed financial decisions.

3. *Employee Productivity:*

    o Leverage data to assess employee productivity and performance. Identify areas for improvement, allocate resources effectively, and enhance overall workforce efficiency.

Customer Relationship Management (CRM):

1. *Personalization and Targeting:*

    o Use customer data to personalize interactions and target marketing efforts. Tailor communications, offers, and experiences based on individual preferences and behaviours.

2. *Churn Prediction:*

    o Analyse customer behaviour to predict and prevent churn. Identify at-risk customers and implement targeted retention strategies to maintain a loyal customer base.

3. *Customer Satisfaction Improvement:*

    o Utilize feedback and satisfaction data to improve customer experiences. Address pain points, enhance customer service, and build long-term relationships.

Continuous Improvement Cycle:

1. *Regular Analysis and Iteration:*

   o Establish a continuous improvement cycle. Regularly analyse data, identify areas for improvement, implement changes, and assess the impact. This iterative process ensures ongoing optimization.

2. *Adaptation to Market Changes:*

   o Use data to monitor market trends and consumer behaviours. Adapt your strategies to align with changing market conditions and evolving customer expectations.

Conclusion

Congratulations on exploring the fundamentals of web analytics tools and understanding how data-driven decisions can significantly impact business performance. In Chapter 12, we will conclude our journey by summarizing key insights and providing actionable takeaways for your business. Keep the momentum going, and may your data-driven approach propel your business to new heights of success!

Chapter 10: Legal and Regulatory Considerations

Understanding and adhering to legal and regulatory frameworks are paramount. This chapter explores key aspects of online business regulations and strategies to protect your business legally.

Understanding Online Business Regulations:

1. *E-commerce Regulations:*

   o Familiarize yourself with e-commerce regulations specific to your jurisdiction. Regulations may cover areas such as online transactions, consumer rights, and electronic contracts.

2. *Data Protection Laws:*

   o Comply with data protection laws, such as the General Data Protection Regulation (GDPR) in the European Union or the California Consumer Privacy Act (CCPA) in the United States. Safeguard customer data and ensure transparent data practices.

3. *Digital Marketing Compliance:*

   o Adhere to regulations governing digital marketing. This includes compliance with anti-spam laws, ensuring transparent advertising practices, and respecting user privacy preferences.

International Considerations:

1. *Cross-Border Transactions:*

   o Understand the legal implications of cross-border transactions. Be aware of tax regulations, import/export restrictions, and compliance with laws in the countries where you operate.

2. *Jurisdictional Compliance:*

   o Navigate jurisdictional complexities by ensuring compliance with the laws of each country in which you conduct business. This includes understanding local tax laws, consumer protection regulations, and business registration requirements.

Protecting Your Business Legally:

1. *Business Structure and Registration:*

   o Choose an appropriate business structure (e.g., LLC, corporation) and register your business according to local regulations. This provides legal protection and defines your business's rights and responsibilities.

2. *Intellectual Property Protection:*

   o Safeguard your intellectual property, including trademarks, copyrights, and patents. Register trademarks for your brand, protect original content, and secure patents for unique inventions or processes.

3. *Terms of Service and Privacy Policies:*

   o Draft comprehensive terms of service and privacy policies for your website or app. Clearly outline user rights, responsibilities, and data usage practices to mitigate legal risks.

Contractual Agreements:

1. *Vendor and Partner Agreements:*

   o Establish clear contractual agreements with vendors and partners. Define terms, responsibilities, and dispute resolution mechanisms to protect your business interests.

2. *User Agreements:*

   o Implement user agreements that outline the terms of use for your platform. Include clauses related to acceptable behaviour, content usage, and consequences for violations.

Compliance with Consumer Protection Laws:

1. *Transparent Pricing and Policies:*

   o Ensure transparency in pricing and policies. Comply with consumer protection laws by providing clear information about product prices, shipping costs, and return policies.

2. *Customer Communication:*

   o Adhere to regulations related to customer communication. Avoid deceptive advertising, provide accurate product information, and obtain proper consent for marketing communications.

Cybersecurity Measures:

1. *Data Security Protocols:*

   o Implement robust cybersecurity measures to protect customer data. Encrypt sensitive information, regularly update security protocols, and monitor for potential vulnerabilities.

2. *Incident Response Plan:*

   o Develop an incident response plan to address potential data breaches or cybersecurity incidents. Outline steps to investigate, mitigate, and notify affected parties in accordance with legal requirements.

   o

Compliance Audits:

1. *Regular Compliance Checks:*

   o Conduct regular compliance audits to ensure ongoing adherence to legal and regulatory requirements. Stay informed about updates to laws and adjust your practices accordingly.

2. *Legal Counsel:*

   o Seek legal counsel to stay informed about changes in regulations and obtain guidance on compliance matters. A legal professional can provide tailored advice based on your specific business context.

Social Responsibility and Ethical Business Practices:

1. *Environmental Impact:*

   o Consider the environmental impact of your business operations. Adhere to environmental regulations, adopt sustainable practices, and communicate your commitment to corporate social responsibility.

2. *Ethical Marketing:*

- o Practice ethical marketing by avoiding deceptive tactics, respecting customer privacy, and ensuring that marketing materials align with your actual products or services.

Crisis Management and Legal Preparedness:

1. *Crisis Communication Plan:*

- o Develop a crisis communication plan to address legal issues or public relations crises. Outline strategies for transparent communication, resolution, and rebuilding trust.

2. *Legal Preparedness Training:*

- o Train your team on legal preparedness. Ensure that key team members are familiar with legal requirements, crisis management procedures, and communication protocols.

Conclusion

Congratulations on navigating the complex landscape of legal and regulatory considerations for online businesses. In this final chapter, we've covered the importance of understanding online business regulations, protecting your business legally, and embracing social responsibility. As you continue your entrepreneurial journey, stay vigilant, stay informed, and uphold ethical standards to ensure the long-term success and sustainability of your online business. Best of luck!

Chapter 11: Scaling Your Business

Scaling a business involves deliberate strategies, smart decisions, and the effective use of resources. This chapter explores key strategies for business growth, the role of outsourcing and automation, and considerations for successful scaling.

Strategies for Business Growth:

1. *Market Expansion:*

   o Identify new market opportunities and geographical areas for expansion. Conduct market research to understand demand, competition, and cultural nuances.

2. *Product Diversification:*

   o Introduce new products or services to diversify your offerings. Analyse customer needs and market trends to develop complementary products that align with your brand.

3. *Customer Retention:*

   o Prioritize customer retention alongside acquisition. Implement loyalty programs, personalized experiences, and excellent customer service to foster long-term relationships.

Strategic Partnerships and Alliances:

1. *Identifying Strategic Partners:*

   o Seek strategic partnerships with businesses that complement your goals. Collaborate with partners to access new markets, share resources, and enhance your overall value proposition.

2. *Joint Ventures and Alliances:*

   o Explore joint ventures and alliances for mutual benefit. Combine strengths with other businesses to achieve shared objectives, whether in marketing, product development, or distribution.

Outsourcing and Automation:

1. *Identifying Tasks for Outsourcing:*

   o Evaluate your business processes and identify tasks that can be outsourced. This may include non-core functions such as customer support, data entry, or certain aspects of production.

2. *Benefits of Outsourcing:*

   o Enjoy cost savings, increased efficiency, and access to specialized skills by outsourcing tasks. Focus on core competencies while delegating routine or time-consuming activities to external experts.

3. *Implementing Automation:*

   o Integrate automation tools for repetitive and rule-based tasks. Automation can streamline workflows, reduce errors, and free up human resources for more strategic activities.

Technology Integration:

1. *Cloud-Based Solutions:*

   o Embrace cloud-based solutions for scalability and flexibility. Cloud computing enables easy access to resources, facilitates collaboration, and allows for rapid adaptation to business needs.

2. *CRM and ERP Systems:*

   o Implement Customer Relationship Management (CRM) and Enterprise Resource Planning (ERP) systems. These tools centralize data, streamline processes, and enhance overall organizational efficiency.

Scaling Considerations:

1. *Financial Planning:*

   o Conduct thorough financial planning to support scaling efforts. Anticipate increased costs, investment requirements, and potential fluctuations in revenue.

2. *Scalable Technology Infrastructure:*

   o Ensure your technology infrastructure is scalable. Choose solutions that can grow with your business and handle increased demands without compromising performance.

3. *Human Resources and Talent Acquisition:*

   o Invest in human resources and talent acquisition to build a skilled and adaptable team. Attracting and retaining top talent is essential for successful scaling.

Customer Feedback and Iteration:

1. *Continuous Improvement:*

   o Gather customer feedback continuously and use it for iterative improvements. A customer-centric approach ensures that your scaling efforts align with market preferences.
2. *Agile Methodology:*

   o Implement agile methodologies in your business processes. Agile practices allow for flexibility, quick adaptation to change, and a focus on delivering customer value.

Monitoring and Analysis:

1. *Key Performance Indicators (KPIs):*

   o Establish and monitor key performance indicators relevant to your scaling objectives. KPIs provide insights into the effectiveness of your strategies and areas for improvement.

2. *Data-Driven Decision-Making:*

- o Base decisions on data analysis. Leverage data to understand customer behaviour, market trends, and the impact of your scaling initiatives on overall business performance.

Risk Management:

1. *Identifying and Mitigating Risks:*

- o Conduct a thorough risk analysis to identify potential challenges associated with scaling. Develop mitigation strategies to address and minimize risks.

2. *Scenario Planning:*

- o Engage in scenario planning to prepare for various outcomes. Anticipate potential challenges and have contingency plans in place to navigate unforeseen circumstances.

Chapter 12: How can A.I. Help Scaling a Business and How Can Do That.

Artificial Intelligence (AI) can play a significant role in scaling a business by introducing efficiency, automation, and data-driven decision-making. Here are several ways AI can contribute to business scalability:

1. *Automation of Repetitive Tasks:*

- o AI-powered automation can handle routine and repetitive tasks, freeing up human resources to focus on more strategic and complex activities. This not only enhances efficiency but also allows the business to scale without a linear increase in labour costs.

2. *Customer Service and Support:*

- o Implementing AI-driven chatbots and virtual assistants can significantly enhance customer service and support. These AI tools can handle a large volume of inquiries, provide instant responses, and even assist with transactional processes, allowing businesses to scale their customer service capabilities.

3. *Data Analysis and Insights:*

   o AI algorithms can analyse vast amounts of data quickly and provide valuable insights. This data-driven decision-making enables businesses to identify trends, customer preferences, and areas for improvement. The insights gained from AI can inform strategic decisions for scaling operations.

4. *Personalization and Customer Experience:*

   o AI enables businesses to deliver personalized experiences to customers. Machine learning algorithms can analyse customer behaviour and preferences to offer tailored recommendations, personalized marketing messages, and a more customized overall experience. This personalization can contribute to customer retention and business growth.

5. *Predictive Analytics:*

   o AI's predictive analytics capabilities help businesses anticipate future trends, demand patterns, and potential challenges. By leveraging predictive models, businesses can make proactive decisions, optimize inventory, and plan for scaling with a forward-looking approach.

6. *Supply Chain Optimization:*

   o AI can optimize supply chain operations by predicting demand, optimizing inventory levels, and improving logistics. This is particularly beneficial for businesses involved in manufacturing or retail, enabling them to scale their operations efficiently.

7. *Marketing and Advertising:*

   o AI can enhance marketing efforts by automating targeted advertising, optimizing ad placements, and analyzing the effectiveness of marketing campaigns. This targeted approach not only improves the efficiency of marketing spend but also allows businesses to scale their promotional activities.

8. *Human Resources and Recruitment:*

   o AI tools can streamline the recruitment process by automating resume screening, identifying suitable candidates, and even conducting initial interviews. This accelerates the hiring process, allowing businesses to quickly scale their workforce when needed.

9. *Cybersecurity and Fraud Prevention:*

   o As businesses scale, the risk of cybersecurity threats and fraud increases. AI-powered cybersecurity tools can monitor and detect unusual activities, identify potential threats, and enhance overall cybersecurity measures, ensuring the security of business operations.

10. *Process Optimization:*

   o AI can optimize internal business processes by identifying inefficiencies and proposing improvements. Whether it's streamlining workflows, automating document processing, or enhancing collaboration, AI contributes to the overall efficiency and scalability of business operations.

To incorporate AI into a business for scalability, consider the following steps:

- Assess Business Processes: Identify areas where AI can bring the most value by automating tasks, improving decision-making, or enhancing customer experiences.

- Choose Relevant AI Solutions: Select AI tools and technologies that align with your business needs. This might include chatbots, machine learning models, predictive analytics software, or other AI applications.
- Integrate AI into Existing Systems: Ensure seamless integration of AI solutions into existing business systems and processes. Collaboration between IT and business teams is crucial for a successful implementation.

- Provide Training and Support: Train employees on using AI tools and provide ongoing support. A smooth transition to AI-powered processes requires proper training and change management.

- Monitor and Evaluate: Regularly monitor the performance of AI applications, analyse their impact on business operations, and make adjustments as needed. Continuous improvement is key to maximizing the benefits of AI for scalability.

By leveraging AI strategically, businesses can not only scale more efficiently but also gain a competitive edge in today's dynamic and technology-driven business environment.

Chapter 13: Final Conclusions

Congratulations on reaching the final chapter of this comprehensive guide to starting and scaling an online business. Throughout this journey, we've explored various facets of entrepreneurship, from the initial ideation phase to the strategies for scaling a thriving business. Let's recap the key takeaways and encourage you, the reader, to take impactful action.

Key Takeaways:

1. Foundations of Online Business:

   - Understand the fundamental principles of online business, including market research, identifying a niche, and establishing a strong online presence.

2. *E-commerce Essentials:*

   - Master the essentials of setting up an online store, choosing the right e-commerce platform, and optimizing the customer shopping experience.

3. *Digital Marketing Strategies:*

   - Dive into effective digital marketing strategies, covering SEO, social media, email marketing, and content marketing to enhance your online visibility.

4. *Customer Relationship Management:*

   o Prioritize customer relationships by offering excellent customer service, personalization, and loyalty programs.

5. *Legal and Regulatory Considerations:*

   o Understand the importance of compliance with online business regulations, data protection laws, and ethical business practices.

6. *Scaling Your Business:*

   o Explore strategies for business growth, the role of strategic partnerships, and the integration of automation and AI in scaling operations.

7. *Analytics and Data-Driven Decisions:*

   o Harness the power of analytics and data-driven decision-making to optimize business performance and stay ahead in a dynamic digital landscape.

8. *Protecting Your Business:*

   o Safeguard your business legally by understanding and complying with regulations, protecting intellectual property, and implementing robust cybersecurity measures.

Encouragement to Take Action:

1. *Reflect on Your Business Journey*:

   o Take a moment to reflect on the knowledge gained throughout this guide. Consider how each chapter contributes to your understanding of building and scaling a successful online business.

2. *Create an Action Plan:*

   o Develop a personalized action plan based on the insights gained. Identify specific areas for improvement, prioritize initiatives, and set measurable goals for your business.

3. *Implement Key Strategies:*

   o Start implementing key strategies immediately. Whether it's enhancing your online presence, refining marketing campaigns, or exploring new partnerships, take tangible steps toward business growth.

4. *Embrace Continuous Learning:*

   o The business landscape is dynamic, and ongoing learning is crucial. Stay informed about industry trends, emerging technologies, and changes in regulations to adapt and innovate.

5. *Build a Support Network:*

   o Surround yourself with a network of mentors, peers, and industry experts. Share experiences, seek guidance, and collaborate with others on the entrepreneurial journey.

6. *Stay Resilient and Adaptable:*

   o Entrepreneurship is a journey filled with challenges and opportunities. Cultivate resilience, adaptability, and a growth mindset to navigate uncertainties and evolve with the changing business landscape.

Final Words:

As you embark on your online business journey or continue to scale your existing venture, remember that success is a culmination of strategic decisions, continuous learning, and a commitment to delivering value to your customers. Your entrepreneurial spirit is a powerful force, capable of driving innovation and making a positive impact.

Thank you for joining us on this exploration of the world of online business. May your entrepreneurial endeavours be marked by success, fulfilment, and a lasting legacy in the digital landscape.

Best wishes for a prosperous and rewarding business journey!